D0903925

The sight of [that pony] did something to me I've never quite been able to explain. He was more than tremendous strength and speed and beauty of motion. He set me dreaming.

—WALT MOREY

THE
HORSE
NOTEBOOK

Albino

Experienced riders are not prone to brag. And usually newcomers, if they start out being boastful, end up modest.

—C.J.J. MULLEN

It is not enough for a man to know how to ride; he must know how to fall.

—MEXICAN PROVERB

North Star

*God forbid that I should go to any heaven
in which there are no horses.*

—R.B. CUNNINGHAME GRAHAM

*A lovely horse is always an experience . . . It is an emotional experience
of the kind that is spoiled by words.*

—BERYL MARKHAM

Andalusian

We kept him until he died . . . and sat with him during the long last minutes when a horse comes closest to seeming human.

—C.J.J. MULLEN

Breton

A horse gallops with his lungs,
Perseveres with his heart,
And wins with his character.

—TESIO

A Hibernian sage once wrote that there are three things a man never forgets—the girl of his early youth, a devoted teacher, and a great horse.

—C.J.J. MULLEN

She was so light on her feet, she danced down the planks and hardly seemed to feel the ground; and she moved with a swaying to and fro of her deer's head in a way to make you think of open moors and flowing airs. The gleaming sun was delighted with her bay coat.

—ERNEST RHYS

Irish Hunter

*. . . An instinct sympathy which makes horse and master one heart, one pulse,
one understanding love—is never made, but born.*

—GEORGE AGNEW CHAMBERLAIN

I will not change my horse with any that treads but on four pasterns . . .
When I bestride him, I soar, I am a hawk. He trots the air, the earth sings
when he touches it, the barest horn of his hoof is more musical than the pipe
of Hermes.

—WILLIAM SHAKESPEARE

It was quite customary as late as 1890 to see a countryman returning from the market, fast asleep, slumped forward over his saddle bar while his horse plodded his own way home.

—DOROTHY HARTLEY

Belgian Heavy Draft

The wagon rests in winter, the sleigh in summer, the horse never.

—YIDDISH PROVERB

Horse, thou art truly a creature without equal, for thou fliest without wings and conquerest without sword.

—THE KORAN

Arab

All our best horses have Arab blood, and once in a while it seems to have come out strong and show in every part of the creature, in his frame, his power, and his wild, free, roving spirit.

—ERNEST THOMPSON SETON

I purchased some classics on horse care . . . I gradually came to understand they were like 19th-century religious tomes on how to save your soul: objective, good; instructions, extremely detailed; practical application, impossible.

—C.J.J. MULLEN

Care, and not fine stables, makes a good horse.
—DANISH PROVERB

Dülmen

Schweiken

My early riding days were spent on the wooden, or rocking variety of mount. Armchairs, bedsteads, all served in my apprenticeship—in fact, my parents' furniture still bears the mark of my whip and improvised spurs!

—ALAN OLIVER

One of the earliest religious disappointments in a young girl's life devolves upon her unanswered prayer for a horse.

—PHYLLIS THEROUX

What a horse does under compulsion is done without understanding, and there is no beauty in it either, any more than if one should whip or spur a dancer.

—XENOPHON

Iceland

It takes all the dignity out of a horse to make him do tricks. Why, a trick horse
is kind of like an actor—no dignity, no character of his own.

—JOHN STEINBECK

Dartmoor

Go anywhere in England where there are natural, wholesome, contented and really nice English people; and what do you always find? That the stables are the real centre of the household.

—GEORGE BERNARD SHAW

If you have it, it is for life. It is a disease for which there is no cure. You will go on riding even after they have to haul you onto a comfortable wise old cob, with feet like inverted buckets and a back like a fireside chair.

—MONICA DICKENS

Brushes in hand, I would wait a while. At last, the mothers, seeing I was harmless, resumed grazing, while I stood up, crept nearer, and began to work. A large, fattish brush for the sky, another for the moor. How simple the whole thing was at that scale—how much better the result! The ponies, the little foals with white legs, made designs at whichever angle I approached.

—SIR ALFRED MUNNINGS

Connemara Pony

*There is something about the outside of a horse
that is good for the inside of a man.*
—SIR WINSTON CHURCHILL

*A good rider on a good horse is as much above himself and others
as the world can make him.*

—LORD HERBERT

It's hard enough to strike off at a canter from a walk with one horse. But to have eight horses doing this at the same time without the slightest raggedness is a work of art.

—VISITOR TO THE SPANISH
RIDING SCHOOL, VIENNA

Lipizzaner

Even the most forlorn thoroughbred, seen at a distance—like a woman outside the fence at an Army camp—is flawlessly beautiful.

—JOE FLAHERTY

Hanoverian

You cannot judge of the horse by the harness.

—PROVERB

We dominate a horse by mind over matter.
We could never do it by brute strength.
—MONICA DICKENS

Noriker

See to it that the colt be kind, used to the hand, and fond of man.

—XENOPHON

Smoothness of execution in every detail is the sine qua non of good horse-manship; jumping in particular, in itself a violent effort, should be rendered as easy and as pleasant as possible for both horse and man by every means in our power.

—PIERO SANTINI

On arriving somewhere in the approximate area of take-off, I let the horse take command and jump the fence. I try to be an uninterfering passenger from there to the other side, and then I take up command again.

—DAVID BROOME

Freiberger

Many persons have sighed for the "good old days" and regretted the "passing of the horse," but today, when only those who like horses own them, is a far better time for horses.

—C.W. ANDERSON

Morgan

Never give up. For fifty years they said the horse was through.
Now look at him—a status symbol.

—FLETCHER KNEBEL

An extra pressure, a silent rebuke, an unseen praising, a firm correction: all these passed between us as through telegraph wires.

—CHRISTILOT HANSON BOYLEN

Carthusian

The rhythm of the ride carried them on and on, and she knew that the horse
was as eager as she, as much in love with the speed and air and freedom.

—GEORGESS McHARGUE

Pinto

Cowboying requires real knowledge of a horse and his capabilities . . . A horse can sense when a real horseman is in the saddle. He knows when the rider is going to tough it out.

—ROBERT REDFORD

A good horse knows just when to turn a cow, just how to cut a steer from the bunch. A good cow pony knows, as if by instinct, when to walk slowly through the brush, how to miss the gopher hole at a high canter. Many a cowboy owes his very life to his horse. The cowpoke and the cow pony become not just a team working in unison, they become as one.

—ROYAL B. HASSRICK

Palomino

No ride is ever the last one. No horse is ever the last one you will have.
Somehow there will always be other horses, other places to ride them.

—MONICA DICKENS

The grandstand was empty and quiet, with the cool feel of an aluminum mixing bowl waiting for ingredients.

—BILL BARICH

You're only a boy, but if you break this colt, you'll be a man—a young man, but a man.

—LINCOLN STEFFENS

American Saddle Horse

Just grab tight with your knees and keep your hands away from the saddle, and if you get throwed, don't let that stop you. No matter how good a man is, there's always some horse can pitch him. You just climb up again before he gets to feeling smart about it. Pretty soon, he won't throw you no more, and pretty soon, he can't throw you no more.

—JOHN STEINBECK

*In buying a horse or taking a wife, shut your eyes tight
and commend yourself to God.*

—TUSCAN PROVERB

Karabair

The horse is God's gift to Man.
—ARABIAN PROVERB

It is best not to swap horses while crossing the river.

—ABRAHAM LINCOLN

. . . But why discourse
Upon the Virtues of the Horse?
They are too numerous to tell
Save when you have a Horse to Sell.

—JOSH BILLINGS

People talk about size, shape, quarters, blood, bone, muscle, but for my part, give me a hunter with brains: he has to take care of the biggest fool of the two and think for both.

—G.J. WHYTE-MELVILLE

Fjord

You can lead a horse to water, but if you can teach him to roll over and float on his back, then you got something.

—JOE E. LOUIS

When I was a young girl, I thought of being a mounted policewoman, because I figured I could ride horses and be paid for it—what a job!

—OLIVIA NEWTON-JOHN

The hooves of the horses!—Oh! witching and sweet
Is the music earth steals from the iron-shod feet;
No whisper of lover, no trilling of bird,
Can stir me as hooves of the horses have stirred.

—WILL H. OGILVIE

Not for nothing has racing been called the sport of kings. Where is such majesty? Where such fleetness? Where such uncertainty? The thrill as the starter pulls the lever and the tapes fly up, and "They're off!" rings from a thousand throats.

—DONN BYRNE

Noram

The race is not always to the swift, nor the battle
to the strong—but that's the way to bet.

—DAMON RUNYON

Thoroughbred

A hundred yards away I saw a big bony colt acting up. He'd just returned from a gallop and was feeling good. He pranced along with that challenging winner's gait. Thoroughbreds are athletes and they probably share with other athletes the brief period of illumination that follows a satisfying workout.

—BILL BARICH

I am still under the impression there is nothing alive quite so beautiful as a thoroughbred horse.

—JOHN GALSWORTHY

Certain comic effects can be achieved by a brand-new rider, especially a man, who dresses like a fashion model and rides like a tailor.

—C.J.J. MULLEN

Salerno

*I can always tell which is the front end of a horse, but beyond that,
my art is not above the ordinary.*

—MARK TWAIN

The sunshine's golden gleam is thrown
On sorrel, chestnut, bay, and roan;
The horses paw and prance and neigh,
Fillies and colts like kittens play,
And dance and toss their rippled manes
Shining and soft as silken skeins. . . .

—OLIVER WENDELL HOLMES

Tennessee Walking Horse

Show me your horse and I will tell you what you are.
—OLD ENGLISH SAYING

There is no secret so close as that between a rider and his horse.
—ROBERT SMITH SURTEES

Jockeys talked to their mounts with their hands, with their palms and fingers, but only a few rare individuals had flesh fine enough to relay messages in an uninterrupted flow.

—BILL BARICH

Gelderland

Mr. Gilling nodded. "Aye, I never knew such a feller for 'osses. He was never happier than when he was with them . . . Do you know, I can remember years ago when he used to fall out with his missus, he'd come down to this stable of a night and sit among his 'osses. Just sit here for hours on end looking at 'em and smoking."

—JAMES HERRIOT

Hackney

My father was, and is, a law-abiding citizen of the realm, but if ever he wanders off the path of righteousness, it will not be gold or silver that enticed him, but, more likely, I think, the irresistible contours of a fine but elusive horse.

—BERYL MARKHAM

Swedish Warm-Blood

Horses and jockeys mature earlier than people—which is why horses are admitted to race tracks at the age of two, and jockeys before they are old enough to shave.

—DICK BEDDOES

A golden bit does not make the horse any better.
—PROVERB

Dog lovers hate to clean out kennels.
Horse lovers like cleaning stables.

—MONICA DICKENS

Shetland Pony

I ate, lived and slept horses. I used to love even the smell of the tack—cleaned, oiled, and shined to an old burnished shimmer.

—CHRISTILOT HANSON BOYLEN

One key to getting along well with a horse is to view him as a fellow creature rather than as an object for entertainment.

—PATRICIA JACOBSON
and MARCIA HAYES

Paso Fino

They say princes learn no art truly, but the art of horsemanship. The reason is, the brave beast is no flatterer. He will throw a prince as soon as his groom.

—BEN JONSON

It may be broadly stated that, with the single exception of goldfish, of all animals kept for the recreation of mankind the horse is alone capable of exciting a passion that shall be absolutely hopeless.

—BRET HARTE

Welsh Cob

Your true horseman may have a great affection for a special pet, but what he loves and reveres from deep down in his being is not a horse but horseflesh— horseflesh as a temple of noble qualities, of endearing foibles, of an astonishing capacity for understanding and cooperation.

—GEORGE AGNEW CHAMBERLAIN

I love the horse from hoof to head,
From head to hoof and tail to mane;
I love the horse, as I have said,
From head to hoof and back again.

—JAMES WHITCOMB RILEY

Good horses make short miles.
—GEORGE HERBERT

Clydesdale

Once the horse bites you, you never get over it.
                                                    —PAUL CLEVELAND

Horses have never hurt anyone yet, except when they bet on them.
—STUART CLOETE

Trakehner

Sometimes they suddenly start racing in the middle of the night, a thudding stampede for no reason, unless it is ghosts.

—MONICA DICKENS

Mustang

Hast thou given the horse strength? hast thou clothed his neck with thunder?

Canst thou make him afraid as a grasshopper? the glory of his nostrils is terrible.

He paweth in the valley, and rejoiceth in his strength: he goeth on to meet the armed men.

He mocketh at fear, and is not affrighted; neither turneth he back from the sword.

—JOB 39: 19 through 22

*There's nothing like a rattling ride
For curing melancholy!*
—WINTHROP MACKWORTH PRAED

Up a hill hurry not,
Down a hill flurry not,
On level ground spare him not.

—ON A MILESTONE NEAR
RICHMOND, YORKSHIRE

Barb

Never . . . telegraph to your horse how you feel unless you want him to feel the same. No creature is more sensitive to mood than a horse. He will at once recognize fear or impatience on the part of his rider.

—MacGREGOR JENKINS

Quarter Horse

Cowboys hate walking; they really know how to use their horses. They conserve the energy of the horse, treating it like a valuable piece of farm equipment.

—ROBERT REDFORD

That hoss wasn't built to tread the earth,
He took natural to the air,
And every time he went aloft,
He tried to leave me there.
　　　　　—ANONYMOUS TRIBUTE
　　　　　　TO AN UNMANAGEABLE HORSE

I must not forget to thank the difficult horses, who made my life miserable, but who were better teachers than the well-behaved school horses who raised no problems.

— ALOIS PODHAJSKY

Standardbred

Haflinger

Horses do think. Not very deeply, perhaps, but enough
to get you into a lot of trouble.

—PATRICIA JACOBSON
and MARCIA HAYES

Too much thinking was the enemy of instinct, and without instinct riders were nothing.

—BILL BARICH

Riding is a complicated joy. You learn something each time.
It is never quite the same, and you never know it all.

—MONICA DICKENS

*Might my husband also ride him? Then he can see
how lovely it is to sit on a well-trained horse.*

—QUEEN ELIZABETH II

Camargue

Great Horse

A man on a horse is spiritually as well as physically bigger than a man on foot.

—JOHN STEINBECK

It was a horse, yet it looked queer—had something on its back. So that was a man! Something was wrong with it. It walked on its hind legs. And it wasn't half as big as a horse!

—HENRY HERBERT KNIBBS

My horses understand me tolerably well; I converse with them at least four hours every day. They are strangers to bridle or saddle; they live in great amity with me, and friendship to each other.

—JONATHAN SWIFT

Turkoman

A canter is the cure for every evil.
—BENJAMIN DISRAELI

To the Greeks, he was a god of beauty, half wild, half tame.
—MONICA DICKENS

Peneia

His eyes were brilliant; they blazed as though red fire were in them. His nostrils quivered and dilated, his neck was proudly arched. In every line and curve of his body there was a lithe, wild gracefulness, an exultant beauty that was strength and swiftness and freedom.

—HERBERT RAVENEL SASS

When I can't ride anymore, I shall still keep horses as long as I can hobble along with a bucket and a wheelbarrow. When I can't hobble, I shall roll my wheelchair out to the fence of the field where my horses graze, and watch them.

—MONICA DICKENS